by Bobby Lynn Maslen
pictures by John R. Maslen

Scholastic Inc.
New York   Toronto   London   Auckland   Sydney

Beginning sounds for Book 3:

O o – octopus
H h – hat
G g – goat
R r – rabbit

For more Bob Books ask for them at your local bookstore or call: 1-800-733-5572.

No part of this publication may be reproduced in whole or in part, or stored in a retrieval system, or transmitted in any form or by any means, electronic, mechanical, photocopying, recording, or otherwise.

ISBN 0-590-22459-X

Copyright © 1976 by Bobby Lynn Maslen.
All rights reserved. Published by Scholastic Inc., 555 Broadway, New York, NY 10012, by arrangement with Bob Books™ Publications.

20 19 18 17 16 15 14   7 8 9/9

Printed in the U.S.A.   10

First Scholastic printing, October 1994

Dot has a hat.

Dot has a cat.

The cat has a hat.

Dot has a dog. Dog has a hat

Dog has a rag hat.

Sad dog.

Sad Dot. Sad cat.

Dog has on a rag hat.

The End

Also available:

More Bob Books
for Young Readers

Even More Bob Books
For Young Readers